Mighty Machines

TRUCK

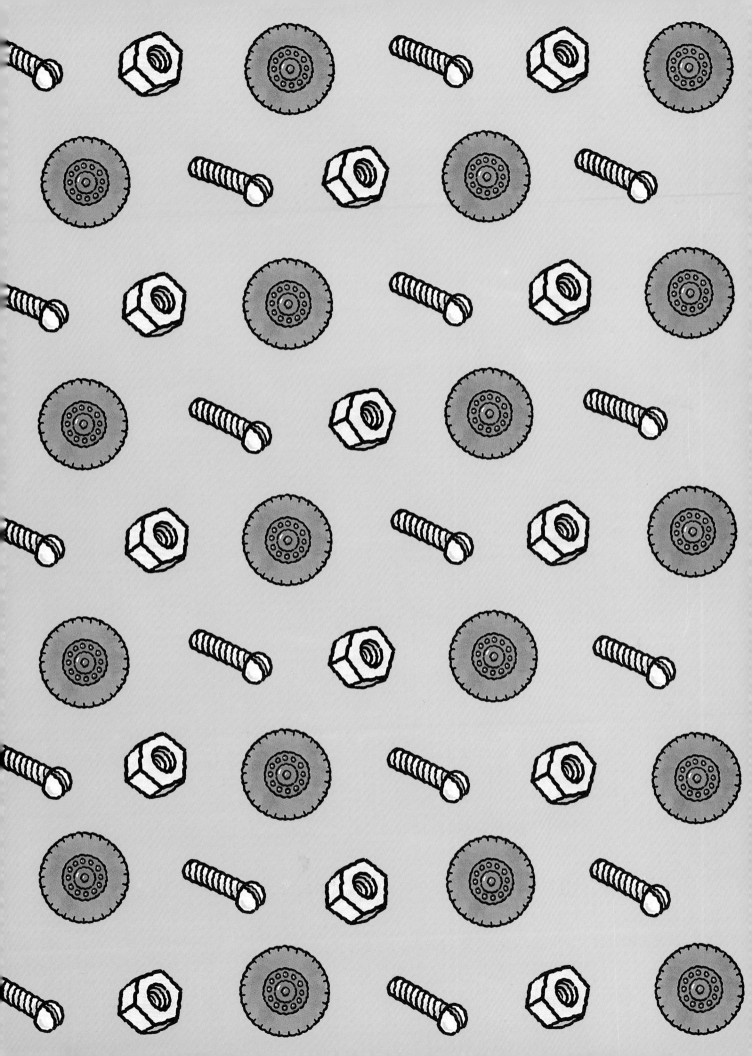

A DORLING KINDERSLEY BOOK
www.dk.com

Editor Miriam Farbey
Designer Helen Melville
Managing Editor Sheila Hanly
Production Josie Alabaster
Photography Mike Dunning,
Richard Leeney
Illustrator Ellis Nadler
Additional photography Finbar Hawkins
Consultant Ian Ogilvie

First published in Great Britain in 1995
by Dorling Kindersley Limited,
9 Henrietta Street, London WC2E 8PS

Paperback edition
2 4 6 8 10 9 7 5 3 1

Copyright © 1995, 1998 Dorling Kindersley Limited

A CIP catalogue record for this book
is available from the British Library.

ISBN: 0-7513-6632-3

Colour reproduction by Chromagraphics, Singapore
Printed and bound in Italy by L.E.G.O.

Dorling Kindersley would like to thank Miller
Mining for their help in producing this book.

The publisher would like to thank the following for
their kind permission to reproduce photographs:
Caterpillar Inc: 19 top
Terex Equipment Ltd: 4 bottom left,
15 top right, 18 top

Scale
Look out for drawings
like this – they show
the size of the machines
compared with people.

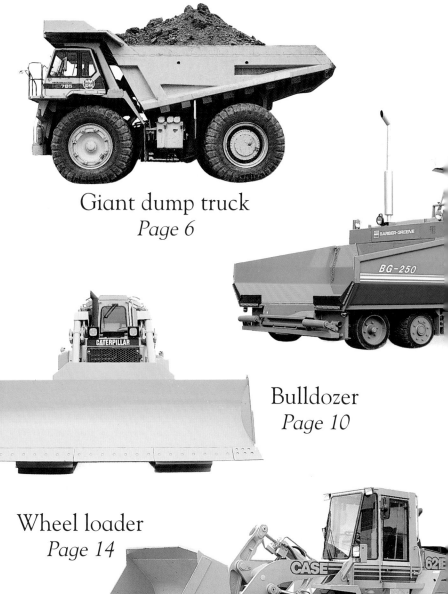

Giant dump truck
Page 6

Bulldozer
Page 10

Wheel loader
Page 14

Scraper
Page 18

Mighty Machines

TRUCK

Claire Llewellyn

DORLING KINDERSLEY
LONDON • NEW YORK • SYDNEY • MOSCOW
www.dk.com

Giant dump truck

The giant dump truck works on the biggest building jobs or in quarries and mines. It carries enormous loads of earth and rock in its body, then tips them out wherever they are needed.

dumper body

Scale

AMAZING FACTS

The truck is 5 metres high, that's higher than two tall adults standing on top of each other.

The dumper body can hold up to 90 tonnes of earth and rock – that's as heavy as 18 elephants.

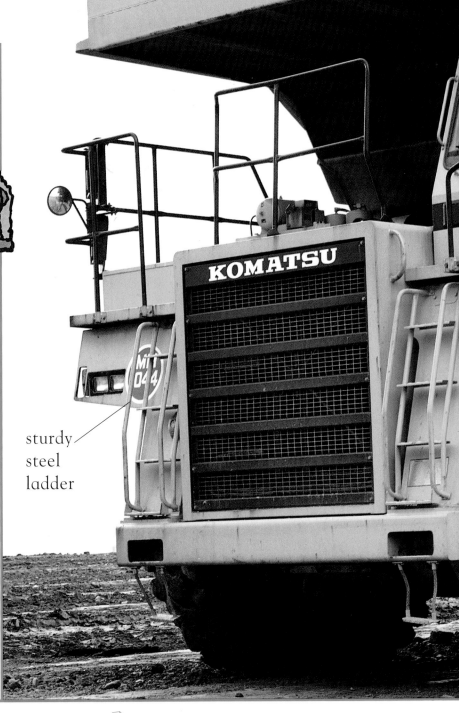

KOMATSU

sturdy steel ladder

The **body** is made out of thick steel. The driver climbs a **ladder** to the cab.

driver sits
in the cab

Tipping out
Sliding arms, called pistons,
lift the body into the air
and the load slides out
with a crash!

heaped
load of
earth

KOMATSU
HD 785
MM 1044

 The **cab** contains the steering wheel, levers, and pedals that control the machine. 7

Mass excavator

The mass excavator is a huge digging machine. It has a long arm with a bucket attached to the end. The bucket scoops out soil or rock and empties it into a dump truck. Different-sized buckets, as well as attachments such as hammers, can be fixed to the arm.

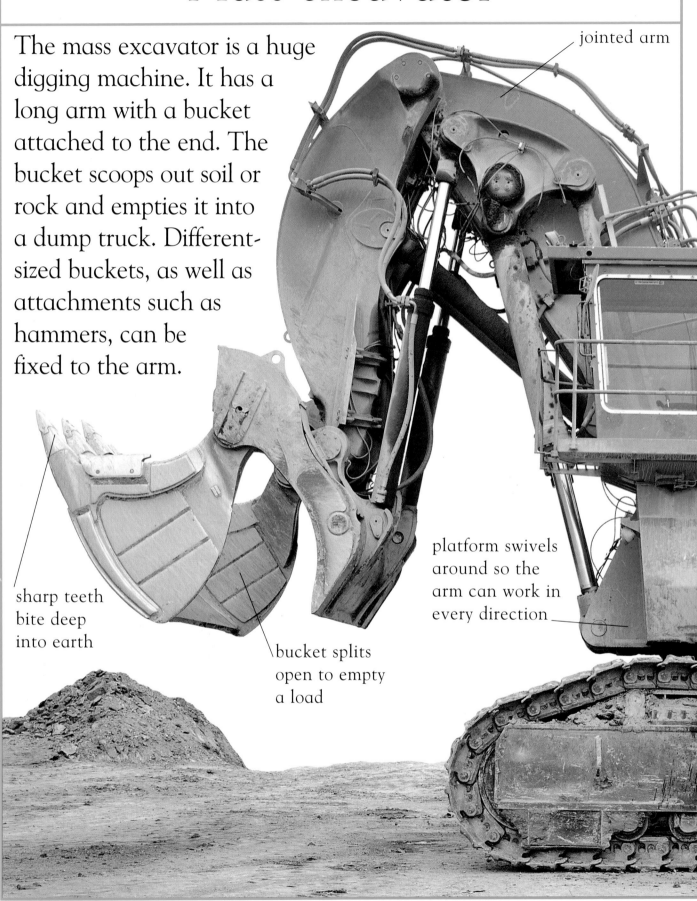

jointed arm

sharp teeth bite deep into earth

bucket splits open to empty a load

platform swivels around so the arm can work in every direction

✎ **Attachments** are tools fixed to a machine. ✎ A **jointed arm** bends like your arm

pistons push
out the arm

machine
crawls on
metal tracks

Track excavator

This excavator is only half the size of the mass excavator. It is used on smaller building sites to dig trenches for pipes, drains, and electric cables.

AMAZING FACTS

A hammer attachment pounds concrete 1,400 times a minute – 20 times faster than you could.

Mass excavators can be 10 metres long – as long as three family cars end to end.

A grapple attachment has claws for picking up scrap.

With the arm stretched out, the machine is 20 metres long – almost as long as a tennis court.

Scale

MM708

K

Metal tracks help machines move smoothly over bumps and grip soft ground.

Bulldozer

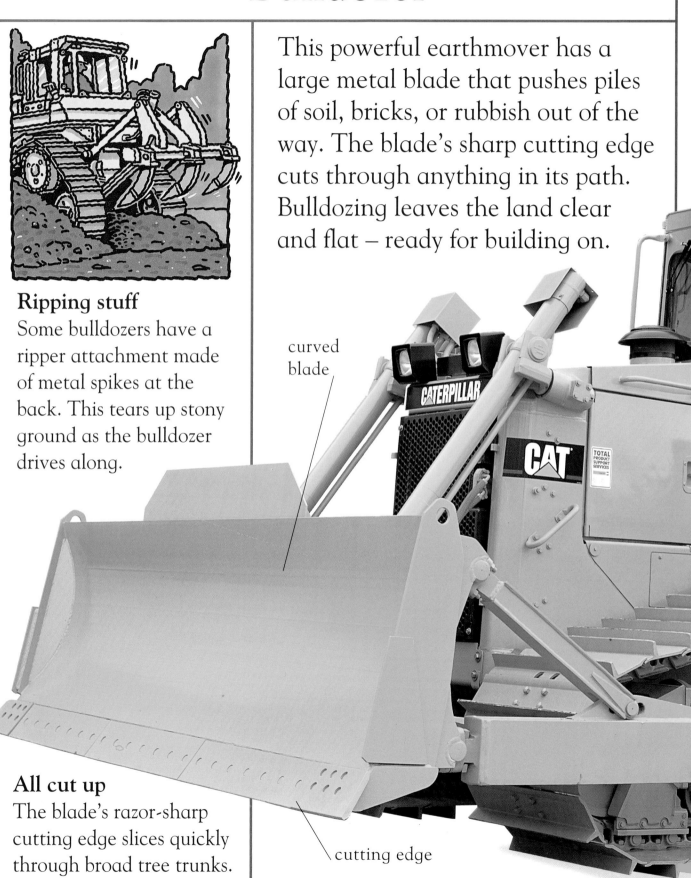

This powerful earthmover has a large metal blade that pushes piles of soil, bricks, or rubbish out of the way. The blade's sharp cutting edge cuts through anything in its path. Bulldozing leaves the land clear and flat – ready for building on.

Ripping stuff
Some bulldozers have a ripper attachment made of metal spikes at the back. This tears up stony ground as the bulldozer drives along.

curved blade

CATERPILLAR

CAT

TOTAL PRODUCT SUPPORT SERVICES

All cut up
The blade's razor-sharp cutting edge slices quickly through broad tree trunks.

cutting edge

Diesel fuel is an oily liquid that is burnt in a vehicle to make it go.

arms tilt
the blade

Up and down
The blade can tilt downwards to cut and push, or upwards to pile up a load of earth.

tank holds
diesel fuel

D6H LGP

strong steel
frame

AMAZING FACTS

⚙ The bulldozer moves as much soil in 3 minutes as you could shovel with a spade in one day.

⚙ The bulldozer weighs 18 tonnes – that's as heavy as 700 seven-year-old children.

⚙ In a tug-of-war, one bulldozer can beat at least 250 people.

⚙ The bulldozer uses 337 litres of diesel fuel in a day's work – that much fuel would last a family car a month.

Scale

Steel is a hard, tough metal made from iron and the chemical carbon.

Backhoe loader

The backhoe loader is two machines in one. At the front is a big shovel for loading up and carrying earth. At the back is a long, powerful arm. Different buckets can be attached to the arm to scoop out trenches for pipes or dig a hole for the foundations of a house.

AMAZING FACTS

🔩 The smallest bucket is 15 centimetres wide – not big enough to catch a beachball.

🔩 The arm can reach to the bottom of rivers 6 metres deep – that's about 20 times deeper than your bath.

Scale

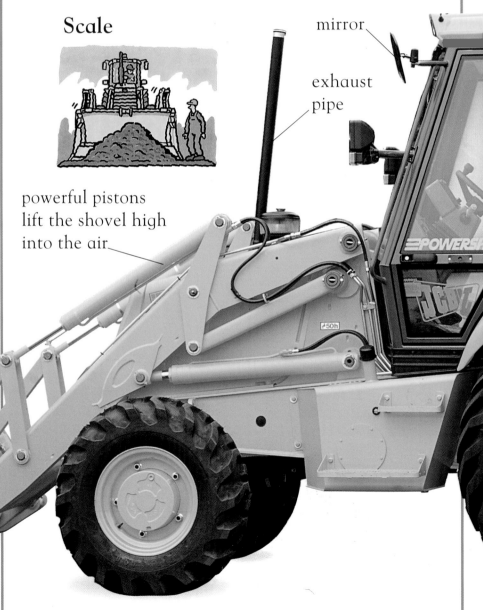

powerful pistons lift the shovel high into the air

mirror

exhaust pipe

🔩 Waste steam and gas are forced out of the engine through the **exhaust pipe**.

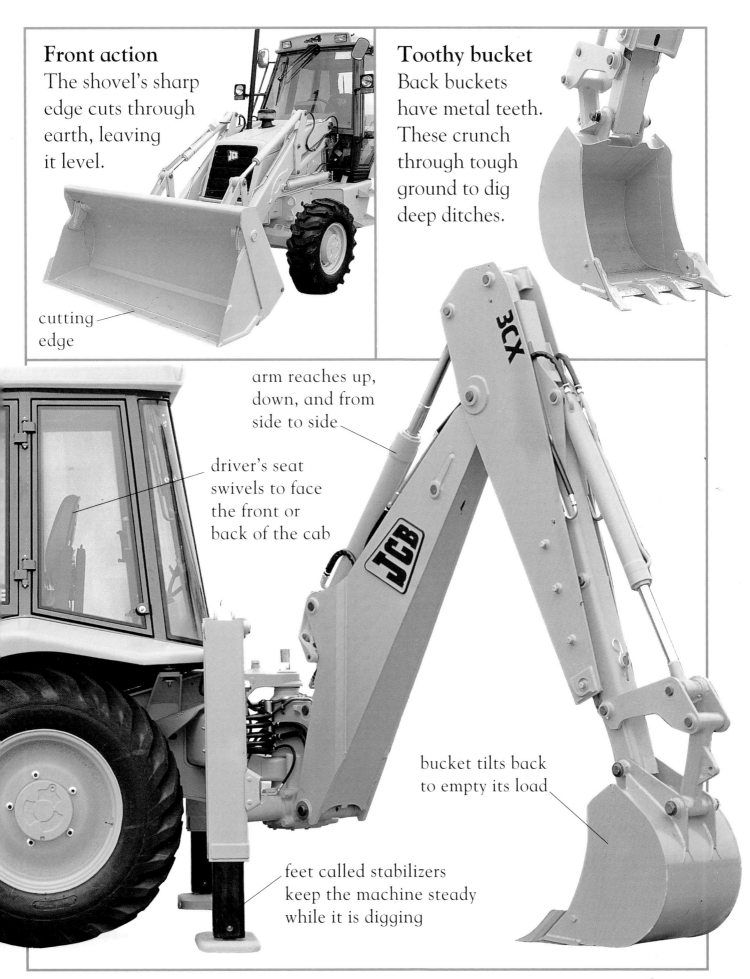

Front action
The shovel's sharp edge cuts through earth, leaving it level.

cutting edge

Toothy bucket
Back buckets have metal teeth. These crunch through tough ground to dig deep ditches.

arm reaches up, down, and from side to side

driver's seat swivels to face the front or back of the cab

bucket tilts back to empty its load

feet called stabilizers keep the machine steady while it is digging

JCB

3CX

Wheel loader

AMAZING FACTS

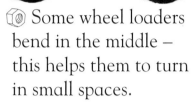

Some wheel loaders bend in the middle – this helps them to turn in small spaces.

The bucket can hold 8 tonnes of sand – as much sand as you would need to build 6,000 sand castles.

The wheel loader is an all-round shovelling, lifting, and loading machine. It works in a lot of places: loading logs on to trucks in a forest, moving sand, gravel, and soil on a building site, or unloading ships at the docks.

Scale

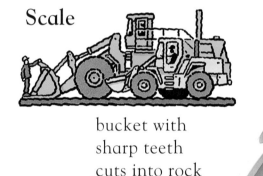

bucket with sharp teeth cuts into rock

arms lift the bucket

The wheel loader weighs over 11 tonnes – that's as much as a bus weighs when it's full of children.

big tyres help the loader to roll smoothly over bumps

A **tyre** is a rubber ring that is fitted round a wheel and filled with air.

Giant wheel loader

This machine is almost ten times bigger than other wheel loaders. It digs out massive chunks of rock in a quarry.

heavy chunk of rock

thick glass helps to keep the cab quiet

621B

ladder has rails at the top to help the driver climb safely

Wood pile

A log grapple can be attached to the loader for stacking logs.

Spill proof

Try to run with a bucket of water. Don't spill any. Loaders carry buckets without spilling a stone.

Stone, slate, or marble for building is cut from the earth's surface in a **quarry**. 15

Moving machines

A site dumper's skip swivels around so it can tip its load out to the left or right.

On bumpy ground, the fork-lift's mast tilts back and forth to balance the load, so it doesn't slide off.

Fork-lifts raise pallets 7 metres high – as high as a two-storey building.

Scale

Fork-lift

You can see fork-lift trucks on building sites or in the warehouse of your local supermarket. Their prongs, or forks, slide into wooden pallets loaded with goods. The pallets are then lifted up the truck's mast and carried wherever they are needed.

mast

long prongs

16 A **pallet** is a wooden tray with two holes through the sides for the fork-lift's prongs.

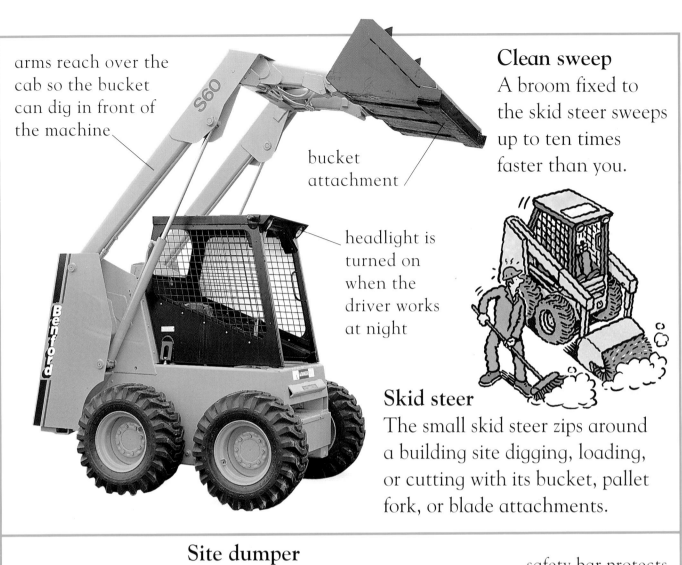

arms reach over the cab so the bucket can dig in front of the machine

bucket attachment

headlight is turned on when the driver works at night

Clean sweep

A broom fixed to the skid steer sweeps up to ten times faster than you.

Skid steer

The small skid steer zips around a building site digging, loading, or cutting with its bucket, pallet fork, or blade attachments.

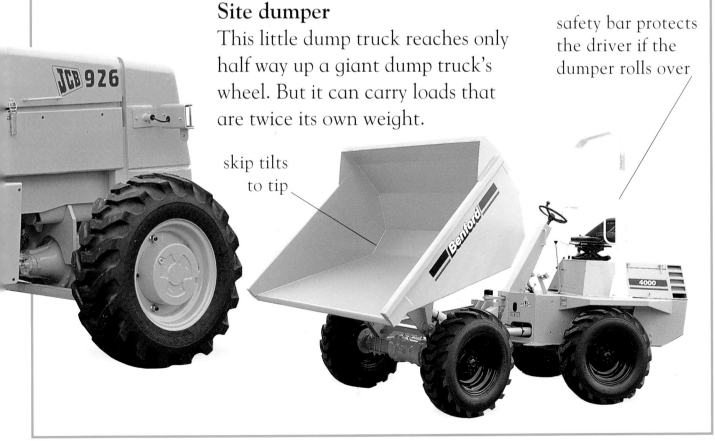

Site dumper

This little dump truck reaches only half way up a giant dump truck's wheel. But it can carry loads that are twice its own weight.

safety bar protects the driver if the dumper rolls over

skip tilts to tip

Road builders

Scraper

The scraper clears the path for a new road. It slices through hills and forests with its sharp blade.

Scale

scraper bowl collects the loose earth

Grader

The metal blade of the grader scrapes the top, bumpy layer off the ground. It makes the earth smooth and level, ready for a road to be laid on it.

Scale

engine

cutting blade

An **engine** turns heat from burning fuel into energy to make a vehicle move.

Scale

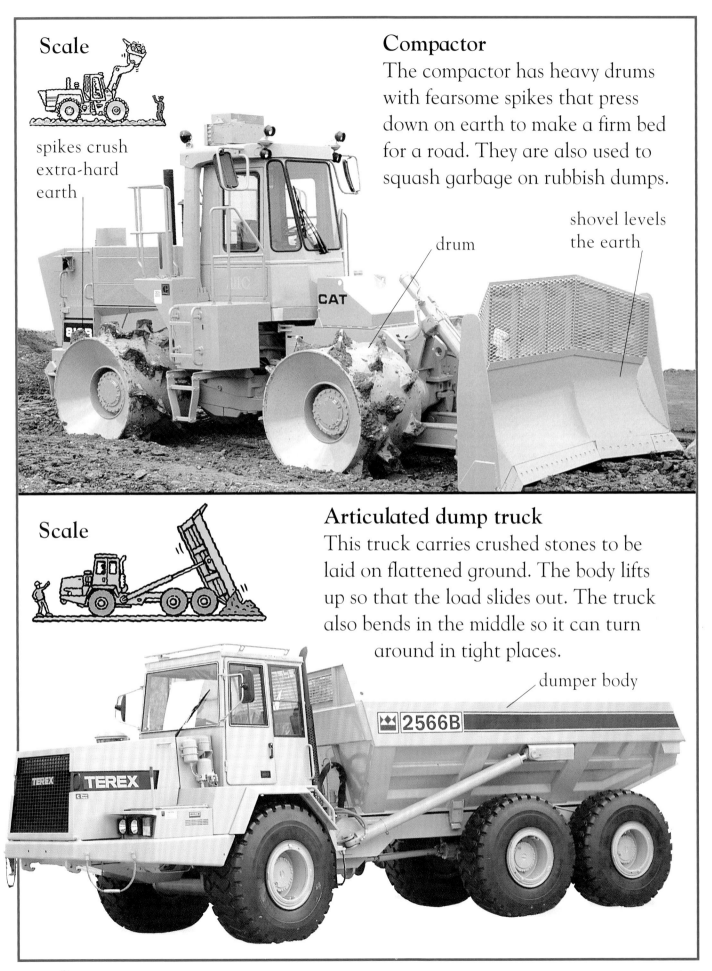

spikes crush
extra-hard
earth

Compactor

The compactor has heavy drums with fearsome spikes that press down on earth to make a firm bed for a road. They are also used to squash garbage on rubbish dumps.

shovel levels
the earth

drum

CAT

Scale

Articulated dump truck

This truck carries crushed stones to be laid on flattened ground. The body lifts up so that the load slides out. The truck also bends in the middle so it can turn around in tight places.

dumper body

2566B

TEREX

An **articulated** vehicle is made of two parts so it can bend in the middle.

Paver and roller

Paver

The paver lays the tarred top surface on new roads. Hot tar and small stones are loaded into the hopper. They pass through the machine and out the back to be spread by a blade, or screed.

canopy protects the driver from the sun

iron screed

hopper

Busybody

One hopperful of tar and stones covers 5 metres of road – you can walk that in six big steps. It takes 12 trucks to load the hopper with enough material to keep the paver busy.

bar is lined with matting to wipe the drum clean

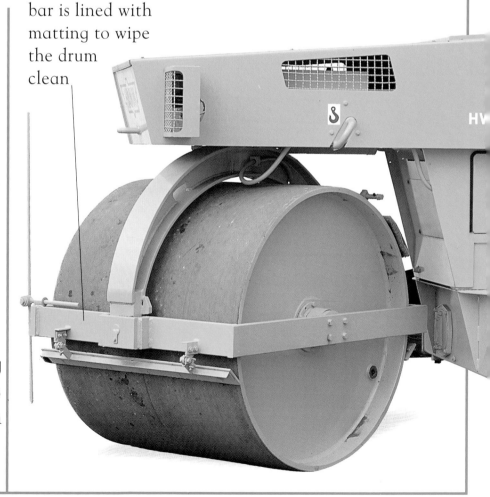

A **hopper** is a square box with a hole at the bottom through which materials pass.

Roller

The roller drives behind the road paver. It has three massive wheels, called drums, filled with water to make them heavy. The drums press down on the tarred surface until it is smooth and flat. Water is sprayed over the drums to cool the hot tar so that it sets and hardens.

AMAZING FACTS

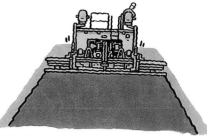

A paver is only 3 metres wide – as wide as three beds. It can pave a road 6 metres wide with extra screeds fixed to its sides.

The paver travels only 1 kilometre in an hour – you can walk backwards more quickly than that.

A roller filled with water weighs 14 tonnes – that's as heavy as 5,000 watermelons.

The roller is over 2 metres wide – wider than five rolling pins laid end to end.

The roller travels at 10 kilometres an hour – as fast as you can cycle.

Scale

steel drum

plug

When the **plug** is pulled out, water flows out of the drum through the plughole. 21